is a Great Big Help!

Psychoanalysis is a new friend

Psychoanalysis
Diploma
of
ZÜRICH

Diploma
PSYCHOLOGY
UNIVERSITY OF
VIENNA

Diploma
Psychology

CASE
HISTORY

Psychoanalysis makes

all things possible

Psychoanalysis is

a Great Big Help!

By Hubert I. Bermont / Drawings by Susan Perl

Psychoanalysis

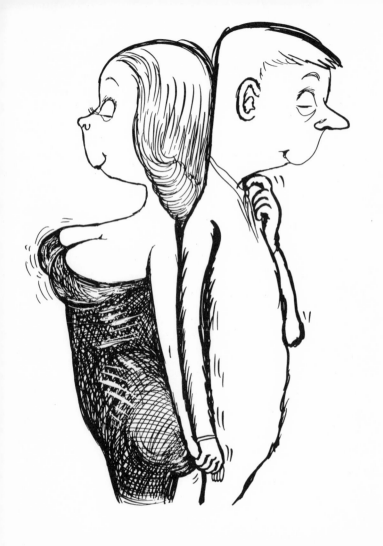

Psychoanalysis enables you

to get along with people

Psychoanalysis helps you

to accept the world as it is

Psychoanalysis brings back

early memories of family life

Psychoanalysis enables you
to come to terms
with your family

Psychoanalysis means coming to terms

with yourself

Psychoanalysis helps you

towards feelings of adequacy

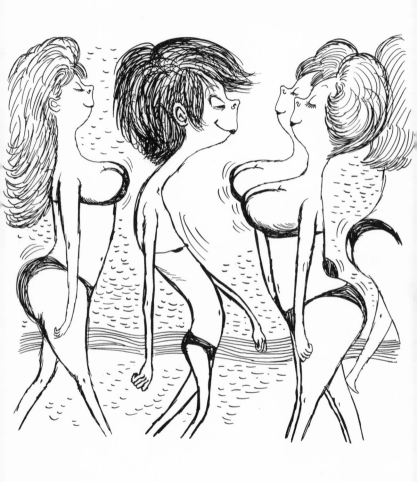

Psychoanalysis enables you
to share
your children's pleasures

Psychoanalysis helps develop

the creative urge

Psychoanalysis is the key

to new pleasure

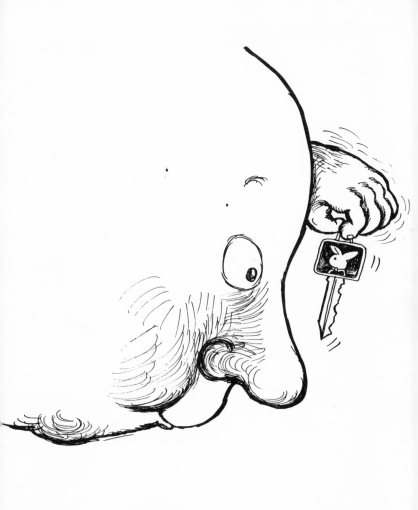

Psychoanalysis gives one

a sense of superiority

Psychoanalysis helps you find

inner peace

Psychoanalysis means
writing down your dreams

Psychoanalysis is an

educational experience

LADIES
ROOM

Psychoanalysis teaches you

about mother love

Psychoanalysis helps you recollect

important impressions

Psychoanalysis enables you

to lose some inhibitions

Group analysis helps you

relate to other people

Psychoanalysis takes a long time

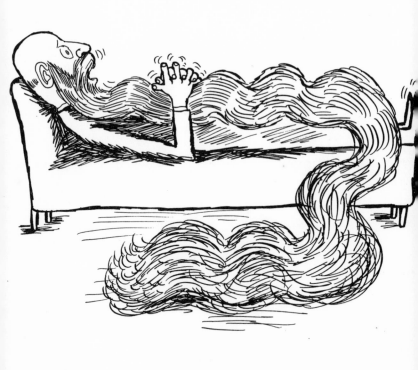

Psychoanalysis cannot channel

all hostility

Psychoanalysis is not

an exact science

Psychoanalysis involves

continued transference

Psychoanalysis doesn't

        really change

your basic character

Psychoanalysis cannot

cure the common cold

Psychoanalysis sometimes

doesn't do a bit of good

Anyway, who's got time for psychoanalysis?